An Iskra Chapbook Series

I0246493

LET US RISE
Trade Unionism in Ireland
Volume 1

Series Editor, *Róisín Dubh*

LET US RISE
Trade Unionism in Ireland
Volume 1

ICELAND: A COLD HOUSE FOR WORKERS
Mícheál Ó Súsleabh and Cristina Diamant

LABOUR IN DUBLIN
James Connolly

THE DUBLIN LOCK OUT
James Connolly

Published by Iskra Books 2023

All rights reserved.
The moral rights of the authors have been asserted.

Iskra Books
WWW.ISKRABOOKS.ORG
US | UK | Ireland

Iskra Books is an independent scholarly publisher—publishing original works of revolutionary theory, history, education, and art, as well as edited collections, new translations, and critical republications of older works.

ISBN-13: 978-1-0880-7857-0

British Library Cataloguing in Publication Data
A catalogue record for this book is available from the British Library

Library of Congress Cataloguing-in-Publication Data
A catalog record for this book is available from the Library of Congress

Cover Art and Design by Ben Stahnke
Typesetting by Róisín Dubh

Contents

Preface \ i
Róisín Dubh

Iceland: A Cold House for Workers \ 1
Mícheál Ó Súsleabh and Cristina Diamant

Labour in Dublin \ 19
James Connolly

The Dublin Lock Out: On the Eve \ 30
James Connolly

*Every effort should be made to extend the scope of public ownership. As democracy invades and captures public powers public ownership will, of necessity, be transformed and infused with a new spirit. As Democracy enters, Bureaucracy will take flight. But without the power of the **Industrial Union** behind it, Democracy can only enter the State as the victim enters the gullet of the Serpent.*

—JAMES CONNOLLY, THE RECONQUEST OF IRELAND

Preface

Róisín Dubh

In 2023, the world witnessed the rise of numerous global labour uprisings. Whether it was the unionisation wave of Starbucks workers in America, or the postal workers in England, the working class—after being treated incredibly poorly during the COVID-19 pandemic—has begun to stand up in record numbers against the exploitive practices of bosses and capitalists. The Irish working class was no exception.

In this new series of *Iskra* chapbooks, we present writings old and new with a focus on the dynamic labor conditions of Ireland. In our inaugural volume, we showcase writings from Iceland[1] grocery workers, who have recently organised themselves, taken strike action, and occupied stores for unpaid wages. In addition

---

1   Iceland Foods Ltd. is a large-scale British supermarket chain, headquartered in Deeside, Wales, operating over a thousand store locations.

to the essay from Iceland workers in the *Independent Workers' Union*, we have also included two relevant pieces written by the Irish trade union leader (among his many other titles), James Connolly.

Even though it has been over 100 years since Connolly wrote about labor conditions in Dublin, there remains a timelessness to his work in the sense that not much, in fact, has changed. Workers continue to endure cost-of-living crises, housing crises, and labour crises.

Without the replacement of capitalism by socialism, without the widescale organisation of laborers and trade unionists, these crises will continue to repeat themselves *ad nauseam* to the detriment of all working class peoples.

It is our hope that *Let Us Rise* will elevate the voices and struggles of those presently engaged in labor actions across Ireland, demonstrating the link and the necessary connection between struggles old and new.

Iceland:
A Cold House for Workers

The Iceland Dispute has demonstrated beyond all doubt what a fighting union can achieve

Mícheál Ó Súsleabh & Cristina Diamant

In February 2023, a group of retail investors met and, over the course of 45 minutes, decided the fate and future of over 300 workers at the Iceland retail chain in Ireland. The refrain we hear from Irish society's optimates is that we should be grateful to live at a time of full employment, and that if we are not happy with it, we can always go somewhere else. The reality is that work in Ireland is becoming meaner and more isolated, and without the protection of trade unions, the majority of people in our country are left completely at the mercy of the whims of suits who think that they are owed a living from the hard work of everyone else. They believe that they are deserving of society and that everyone else has to accommodate themselves to their priorities.

The Irish labour market is suffering from serious instability. Workers in some sectors are also suffering from serious illusions that they are living in a country where their rights are protected by law, and where they will never be at risk of maltreatment or unfair dismissal. Some workers even believe that they are part of the ruling class and will be spared when their livelihood becomes inconvenient for someone else. Our experience tells us different—and a big part of the message and success of the Iceland dispute has been getting the message through that this could happen to anyone. Anyone could wake up in the morning and find a door slammed shut in their face, with bills to pay and a family to feed.

We live in an era of unprecedented mental health crises when people are struggling with learned helplessness—when you are told constantly and repeatedly that you are powerless and have to accept the demands and dictats of the wealthy, it can lead to a dehumanising loss of agency. This state of affairs is actively encouraged by a capitalist class that sees working class people as less than human, and wants to ensure that they can get away with the most with the least resistance. There are no social supports available for people in our atomised neoliberal society. We spend our lives, cradle to grave, working ourselves to the bone in the belief that if we are loyal, productive members of society, we will be recognised and protected. Instead, workers frequently find themselves treated as an afterthought, or worse, as refuse.

The one place where workers can claim back their dignity and unity, find a real sense of community, and assert themselves from a position of real social and economic strength is in a trade union. The majority of the establishment trade unions in Ireland are not interested in such empowerment of ordinary people, because an activist trade union membership can present a threat to the security and interests of senior trade union members. The union structure is unique in that it contains both volunteers and employees, and while there are many dedicated, sincere and morally strong trade unionists operating in every organisation, many have also resigned themselves to putting in time since social partnership—or worse, fooled themselves into thinking that they're running the country.

These are the challenges facing the Irish trade union movement—a class to represent that is disillusioned with the failures of a trade union movement that is unresponsive to their needs, that is been bullied into giving up trying to improve their lot, and has been lulled into a false sense of security by a pale imitation of functioning industrial relations machinery. It was in this context, and in this difficult situation, with many companies exiting the labour market or reducing their workforce that the Independent Workers' Union set out to organise a campaign for workers in 2023.

Dare to Struggle, Fight to Win

When the Independent Workers' Union (IWU) first heard of the issues that workers were experiencing in Iceland stores in March, we immediately dispatched organisers to stores in Dublin. The structure of the Dublin branch had recently been overhauled and there is a new focus on campaigning and investigating any potential leads that might lead to the unionisation of workers facing difficult conditions without support from an existing trade union. While the Iceland stores in Dublin were not unionised, many of the workers had experience through their families and communities of industrial action, and many had previously witnessed the Debenhams dispute where another UK-based company closed all of its Irish options, locking workers out without any appropriate redundancy arrangements.

Many UK businesses have exited the Irish market in similar circumstances in recent years, citing Brexit and regulatory impositions as reasons for closing poorly operating branches and moving to franchise models or exiting entirely. Despite the apparent problem of moving goods across the border in the Irish sea, Iceland appears to have totally changed its business model during the takeover, switching from a distribution system that saw stock arriving overland from the North of Ireland to the South of Ireland, to a system of importation by ship from Liverpool and other port cities to Dublin. Naeem Maniar, an Irish-based Indian businessman, who had previously owned Iceland as a franchisee in Ireland before placing the business into examinership, took over operations for a token price of 1 euro.

Naeem Maniar embarked on immediately downsizing, closing the head office entirely and focusing on cost-cutting. The removal of all centralised administration seems to have backfired badly and shown flagrant disregard for the structural integrity and operational effectiveness of the company. Without closely co-operating administrative staff, there does not appear to have been anyone to notice the problems which were accumulating, including payroll issues with workers going unpaid and not receiving holiday entitlements, importation papers not being checked for validity and appropriate paperwork not being filed with the relevant authorities. Many workers at Iceland attempted to raise these issues with management but were ignored entirely. There was clearly an impetus within Iceland to get as much profit out of the company as possible in the short-term. Leaseholders and suppliers went unpaid, and there is much evidence to suggest that this is a recurring strategy as part of strategic bankruptcy, with the backers behind Maniar running up impossible debts, possibly even stripping assets off the books (an associate of Maniar has been alleged to strip shops which have been shut down due to non-payment of rent and hold the fixtures hostage until a favourable lease termination is arranged), and then running for the safety of examinership by court order protecting them from their creditors.

Of course, the creditor who has sweated the most to keep the company running and stands to lose the most by the destruction of the company is the workers themselves, and in this shady and dodgy dealing, they appear to never have been a consideration or taken seriously by management. After all, there is no incentive for management to pay attention to the needs and wishes of their employees unless they band together and force them to pay attention.

And this is exactly what the Iceland workers did. While the industrial relations machinery and court system in Ireland may offer a potent force for the protection of capital and the interests of businessmen, there is little option for worker to avail of to recover their wages beyond going to the Workplace Relations Commission (WRC), where there is every pressure on them to give up and let go of their hard-earned wages when adjudication can take over a year, and the actual receipt of money from a WRC decision might not come down the line until after eighteen months, while the company harangues and victimises them.

Action Produces Results

Throughout April the IWU focused on organising the workers, building links between its activists and building a rapport at different stores, and carrying out surveys to establish how many workers were owed wages and the amounts involved. During the month, the management shut off air conditioning at several stores to save on electricity builds and workers were forced to work in sweltering 35 degrees Celsius indoors while customers complained and stock spoiled. The IWU made several attempts to contact the new franchisees to enter into negotiations representing its members, but were ignored. In May, with eleven thousand euro owed to workers and several stores having been fully unionised, the IWU balloted its members for strike action. On 19 May 2023, workers at the Coolock and Northside stores walked out in one of the first industrial actions of the year.

They met profound support from a community disgusted at the way they had been treated, and several thousand euros was collected for a solidarity fund from many sources, including other trade unions lending an arm in support. With the owner, Naeem Maniar, running scared to several stores to reassure the workers that conditions would change and improve, it appeared the company had finally gotten the message and things calmed down for several weeks as a slow trickle of money came into workers who had been unpaid. This seems to have been a temporary development of conscience, however. On 16 July 2023, the Food Safety Authority of Ireland (FSAI) carried out a product recall of all animal products sold in Irish Iceland stores. Shortly after, on the 21st of July 2023, Iceland workers throughout the country showed up for work, and in an act of utter disrespect, found their stores closed without any notice to them.

A Better Way is Possible

One of the most positive things to emerge from the Iceland dispute is politicians calling for increased funding for Labour Court inspections and for inspectors to visit stores more frequently to nip distressful working conditions in the bud. It was pointed out that the state had acted quickly to protect consumers from potentially harmful meat products, and to ensure that unlawful importation of goods was not occurring, but it failed to show the same concern or consideration for the hardworking employees who had been disrespected and mistreated by the company. This was no mere oversight: not much seems to have changed since the summer of 2020, when an IWU representative spoke before the Oireachtas[1] about the contrast between the state's immediate concern with consumer safety as opposed to concerns for workers in meat plants notorious for COVID-19 re-infections where unsustainable targets led to repetitive strain injuries and accidents. The neoliberal fantasy stays the same: shelves have to stay

---

1 **Editor's Note:** The *Oireachtas* is the Parliament of Ireland.

consistently stacked, rendering the hands they pass through invisible. These only briefly become visible to the consumers when things do not go according to plan and they have to intervene, correcting rather than anticipating and eliminating issues. Interestingly, the consumers' demographic also played a role in how close the public personally felt to the mistreated Iceland workers: these stores were small operations, without a self-checkout option. Human interaction, however brief, was built into its business model.

The issue needs to be treated as a symptom of a larger, more pervasive issue rather than an irrational exception. To adequately treat it, the regulatory system needs to have more bite, which runs contrary to the model of "social partnership," cloaking the simple fact that employers do not see trade unions as equal partners in the labour market but as a thorn in their side, holding them back from increasing their profit margins at the expense of the employees they treat as a resource easily discarded. This is precisely why simply raising the issue in the Dáil[2] is insufficient: when the law has no teeth by design, political representatives may feign surprise, dodge calls to action with vague promises of further consultation or even claim victimhood for

---

2   **Editor's Note:** The *Dáil*, also known as Leinster House, is the lower house of the Oireachtas.

being put on the spot. The real target is not one representative or another failing constituents, but an entire class pretending not to be actively waging class war.

In 2001, the European Parliament passed the Transfer of Undertakings Directive 2001 which has long since been transposed into Irish domestic legislation. One of the key issues at the heart of the Iceland dispute is that the transfer of undertaking procedures provided for in the domestic legislation on foot of the Transfer of Undertakings Directive 2001 have been totally disregarded. Several of the core stipulations of this legislation, such as workers being informed directly of any change to pay and conditions with ongoing engagement, were totally skipped over. Article 7 of the Transfer of Undertakings Directive 2001 states that employers must consult their employees prior to even considering a transfer of undertakings, and this obviously has not taken place given the total dearth of communication with the workers. EU legislation is frequently held up as a paragon of workers' rights, but the reality is that EU legislation, even where it has been given effect in member state law, is frequently ignored when it favours workers' rights but enacted all too stringently when it favours the bosses. There are numerous examples of CJEU rulings serious affecting the rights of workers, including recent rulings on pay for posted workers, as well as the infamous EU Commission vs. Luxembourg case, C-319/06, where the EU commission leveraged competition law to force down workers' pay and condition. Since then, the IWU through its activity in the meat industry in Ireland has represented a number of agency workers who were falsely posited as being employed by a Polish agency and subject to Polish pay requirements and industrial relations and tax schemes. If EU Law is at all to be taken seriously or put forward as being "progressive" in relation to Labour law, then it has to be totally reconfigured to put real teeth on the violations of its terms and to curtail the pro-capitalist litigiousness of the EU Commission. In Ireland, either the WRC or the Corporate Enforcement Authority urgently require scope to aggressively pursue companies that ignore Transfer of Undertakings (TUPE) legislation, up to and including investigation of sites on foot of complaints by the Labour Court.

When fighting a feature of neoliberalism, however, legislative tools prove inadequate compared to community-led solutions. Petitions can be ignored by decision-making bodies, but phone banking, a strategy successfully employed by other likeminded organisations, such as CATU (Community Action Tenants' Union), disrupts daily operations enough to force the responsible party to at least listen to grievances. Industrial action remains the gold standard at the core of our entire outlook, but we need to move past a restrictive legal environment for this power to again approach its past zenith, and we need to hone and refine our political strategy and interactions with other causes.

Piercing the Corporate Veil

In the aftermath of the beginning of closures, the company filed for examinership, and an examiner was appointed to manage the company's future and find new investors. The company appears to have abused a concept of "temporary layoffs" in the hope that it could avoid paying out any of its obligations with respect to redundancy, and there has been little explanation from the company to the court of how it was going to find an investor after such severe mismanagement and reputational damage. Questions were raised about how its massive debt of 32 million euros to the parent company and Naeem's other concerns had been accumulated, and whether the overall situation of examinership was an attempt to get as much out of the business as possible while avoiding these obligations—in effect, pulling a stroke both on the state and its own employees and business partners.

The whole situation establishes the desperate need for reform of industrial relations and corporate governance structure in Ireland. A number of companies have exited and are planning to exit the Irish market—restrictions and structures should be in place to force companies that are planning to engage in capital flight to pay a fair share to workers who have contributed so much to their profits over so many years. Workers should have an option of first refusal, companies should be required to pay workers as their first priority and should not be allowed to avail of the protection of the courts in the manner that the current examinership system allows. This enables, facilitates, and rewards dishonest behaviour rather than protecting debtors. If someone owes money for their mortgage, they lose their house, if someone owes dozens of millions, they get a write-off and go back to their other profitable businesses and continue their affluent lifestyle, while their workers try to pick up the pieces of their lives.

As outlined in a 30 May 2023 article in the Ditch, Metron Stores Limited in Ireland is a shell company of Project Point Technologies, owned by Naeem Maniar and a mysterious Trust. This layering of companies is popular amongst Irish businesses to insulate owners from any possible responsibility for corporate misdeeds. It has been exploited by Naeem Maniar and others at the Workplace Relations Commission (WRC) to argue that they are not the employer of the Iceland workers, and that it is in fact solely Metron Stores Limited that should be named as the workers' employer. This tenuous legal argument hints at the numerous options available to employers to circumvent their obligations to workers through the corporate veil, the separate personhood and legal identity of businesses. While in common law jurisdictions, judges may sometimes decide to "pierce the corporate veil" where they hold the employer responsible for wrongdoing and require them to shoulder liability for irresponsible decisions, this is rarely seen in practice and is usually only carried out where criminality in other respects is occurring. The result is that fly-by-night companies, and even some larger institutional enterprises, can compartmentalise their company structure and pursue greater risks at limited cost as a result. There will never be an appetite to face down this behaviour and force dishonest actors to accept their social responsibilities without well-organised and sustained pressure from labour unions.

It should speak to the inadequacy of "social partnership" between conventional ICTU trade unions and the state that after nearly 30 years of close collaboration, we are in a weaker position vis-à-vis the capitalist class than we were before, and the calculated exploitation of loopholes in the law obvious to many who encounter them regularly at the WRC continues unchallenged.

An Example for the Future

Several store occupations and a further strike have ensued. The Independent Workers' Union has held rallies outside the occupied Iceland store on Talbot Street and alternated shifts occupying the store with workers and other union members. People from throughout the country have contributed support, both financial and physical, and the effect of rallies has been uplifting in reminding workers that their concerns are important and their contributions are valued. People who otherwise may have been left alone in one of the darkest hours of their lives have instead had the solidarity of the entire community celebrating their struggle with music and camaraderie.

The examiner has been forced to engage with the workers and take account of their lost wages. A new investor has been found, and with hundreds of Iceland workers, now the majority in the entire country, members of the Independent Workers' Union, there is hope that we now have the bargaining position to force the new owners to give their employees the option of relocation to other parts of their business or a serious and substantial redundancy package.

The Iceland dispute has been a microcosm of the wins that can still be achieved, even with all of the power arrayed against our struggle. The current state of the trade union movement in Ireland and the world can be demoralising. It can seem at times like there is no trade union "strategy" to speak of, and that trade unions are playing a subservient role in society. However, by looking the past for inspiration, by studying the triumphs of Connolly and Larkin, and understanding that no worker is ever truly alone, but that we are all members of the same class and working together in the same struggle, we can unlock an unstoppable power. Our role as activists now is to make sure that no one who is marginalised or ignored goes voiceless, but that when there is an injury against one of us, then it is an injury against all. That when a single member of our class is cheated, robbed, or made feel small, that there is a unity that can vindicate them and open the path to a different society. The trade union movement can never be more than one stream in the river of holding power to account and demanding a total renegotiation, not just of employment and industrial relations, but the entire nature of power in a society where class domination has been accepted as the natural way of things.

Mícheál is an independent scholar from Cork, Ireland currently engaged in academic research on the work of Mikhail Suslov.

Cristina Diamant is the current President of the Independent Workers' Union.

Labour in Dublin

First Published in *The Irish Review*
October 1913, Vol. 3, No. 32

James Connolly

Having been asked by the Editor of the *Irish Review* to contribute for this month's issue a statement of the position of Labour in the present crises in Dublin, and having gladly consented, I now find myself to be in somewhat of a difficulty in setting the limits and scope of my article. I know not whether to restrict myself to a simple setting forth of the merits or demerits of the present dispute, and our general view of the history and prospects of that section of the population of Ireland to which we belong, to wit, the Working Class. I would like to do both, but to do either would require not merely an article but a volume in itself. Hence, in whatever there may be of scrappiness or indefiniteness of purpose in the writing of this article, the reader may detect the influence of that doubt as to how much I should attempt, and how much I should leave to other occasions, and perhaps to other pens.

Ireland is a country of wonderful charity and singularly little justice. And Dublin being an epitome of Ireland, it is not strange to find that Dublin, a city famous for its charitable institutions and its charitable citizens, should also be infamous for the perfectly hellish conditions under which its people are house, and under which is men, women and children labour for a living. No need for me to repeat here the tale of the vast proportion of the total families of Dublin who live in homes of one room per family, nor yet to tell of the figures given us year by year by Sir Charles Cameron—figures which drive home the fact that the high death rate of Dublin is in exact proportion to the class to which the victims belong, a death rate falling with the wealth of the people and rising with their poverty. All these things ought to be familiar to every patriot; if they are not, it is a sure sign that their patriotism takes no stock of those things which make for or against the well-being and the greatness of peoples.

But whilst there have been long available statistics of the high rents and poor housing of the

Dublin working class, there have not been, and are not even now available, statistics of the wages and labour conditions of Dublin.

The information which might be supplied to the general public by such statistics has for the most part been left to be gathered piecemeal by the workers themselves, and to be applied piecemeal in an unconnected fashion as it became necessary to use it for purposes of organisation and agitation. Used in such fashion, it was never collected into one co-ordinated whole, as for instance, Mr. Rowntree has given us in his study of the conditions of York, or Mr. Booth in his study of the East End of London. One reason for this neglect of the social conditions of Dublin has been that in Ireland everything connected with the question of poverty insensibly became identified with one side or the other in the political fight over the question of national government. The reform temperament, if I may use such a phrase, could not escape being drawn into the fight for political reform, and the Conservative temperament quite as naturally became a pawn in the game of political reaction. Now it is well to remember that a conservative temperament is not naturally allied to social abuses or industrial sweating, but may be, very often is, the most painstaking of all the elements making for the correction of such abuses within certain limits; it is also well to be clear upon the fact that a readiness to fight or even to die for national freedom might co-exist in the same person with a vehement support of industrial despotism or landlord tyranny. Thus it has happened that all the literary elements of society, those who might have been, under happier political circumstances, the champions of the downtrodden Irish wage labourer, or the painstaking investigators of social conditions, were absorbed in other fields, and the working class left without any means of influencing outside public opinion. As a result, outside public opinion in Dublin gradually came to believe that poverty and its attendant miseries in a city were things outside of public interest, and not in the remotest degree connected with public duties, or civic patriotism. Poverty and misery were, in short, looked upon as evils which might call for the exercise of private benevolence, but their causes were to be looked for solely in the lapses or weaknesses of individual men and women, and not in the temporary social arrangements of an ever-changing industrial order.

In this Dublin, with all this welter of high political ideals and low industrial practices, vaulting Imperialism and grovelling sweating, there arose the working class agitator. First as the Socialist, analysing and dissecting the difference between the principles and practices of the local bosses of the political parties, drawing attention to the fact that wages were lower and rents higher in Dublin than in England, that railwaymen received in Ireland from five shillings to ten shillings per week less for the same work than they did in England, that municipal employees were similarly relatively underpaid, that in private employment the same thing was true, and that the Irish worker had fought everybody's battles but his own. That there was no law upon the Statute Book, no order of the Privy Council, and no proclamation of the Lord Lieutenant which compelled, or sought to compel, Irish employers to pay lower wages than were paid for similar work in England, or Irish house-owners to charge higher rents. That the argument about struggling Irish industries as opposed to wealthy English ones was being used to bolster up firms which had been so long established that their position was as secure as that of any English firm; and yet, sheltering behind this argument, they continued to pay sweating wages of the worst kind.

It was further insisted that as the Irish farmer had only succeeded in breaking the back of Irish landlordism by creating a public opinion which made allegiance to the farmer synonymous with allegiance to Ireland, which treated as a traitor to Ireland all those who acted against the interests of the farmer, so the Irish Working Class could in its turn only emancipate itself by acting resolutely upon the principle that the cause of Labour was the cause of Ireland, and that they who sought to perpetuate the enslavement and degradation of Labour were enemies of Ireland, and hence part and parcel of the system of oppression. That the conquest of Ireland had meant the social and political servitude of the Irish masses, and therefore the re-conquest of Ireland must mean the social as well as the political independence from servitude of every man, woman and child in Ireland. In other words, the common ownership of all Ireland by all the Irish.

Into the soil thus prepared there came at a lucky moment the organisation of the Irish Transport and General Workers' Union. This Union has from its inception fought shy of all theorising or philosophising about history or tradition, but, addressing itself directly to the work nearest its hand, has fought to raise the standard of labour conditions in Dublin to at least an approximation to decent human conditions. To do this it has used as its inspiring battlecry, as the watchword of its members, as the key-word of its message, the affirmation that "an injury to one is the concern of all"—an affirmation which we all admire when we read of it as the enunciation of some Greek or Roman philosopher, but which we are now being asked to abhor when, translated into action, it appears in our midst as "the Sympathetic Strike." I am writing without time to consult my books, but I remember that one of the Wise Men of old, when asked "what was the most perfect state," answered "that in which an injury to the meanest citizen was considered as an outrage upon the whole body." And the reply has come down the ages to us as the embodiment of wisdom. Is it an illustration of the conflict between our theories and our conduct that the lowest paid, least educated body of workers are the only people in Ireland who try to live up to this ideal, and that this attempt of theirs should lead to their being branded as outlaws?

What is the Sympathetic Strike? It is the recognition by the Working Class of their essential unity, the manifestation in our daily industrial relations that our brother's fight is our fight, our sister's troubles are our troubles, that we are all members one of another. In practical operation, it means that when any body of workers are in conflict with their employers, that all other workers should cooperate with them in attempting to bring that particular employer to reason by refusing to handle his goods. That in fact every employer who does not consent to treat his workpeople upon a civilised basis should be treated as an enemy of civilisation, and placed and kept outside the amenities and facilities offered by civilised communities. In other words, that he and his should be made "tabu" [taboo], treated as unclean, as "tainted," and therefore likely to contaminate all others. The idea is not new. It is as old as humanity. Several historical examples will readily occur to the mind of the thoughtful reader. The *Vehmgerichte* of Germany of the Middle Ages, where the offending person had a stake driven into the ground opposite his door by orders of the secret tribunal, and from that moment was as completely cut off from his fellows as if he were on a raft in mid-ocean, is one instance. The boycott of Land League days is another. In that boycott the very journals and politicians who are denouncing the Irish Transport Union used a weapon which in its actual operations was more merciless, cruel and repulsive than any Sympathetic Strike has ever yet been. And even the Church, in its strength and struggles when it was able to command obedience to its decrees of excommunication, supplied history with a stern application of the same principle which, for thoroughness, we could never hope to equal. Such instances could be almost indefinitely multiplied. When the peasants of France rose in the Jacquerie against their feudal barons, did not the English nobles join in sympathetic action with those French barons against the peasantry, although at that moment the English were in France as invaders and despoilers of the territory of those same French feudal barons? When the English peasantry revolted against their masters, did not all English aristocrats join in sympathetic action to crush them? When the German peasantry rose during the Reformation, did not Catholic and Protestant aristocrats cease exterminating each other to join in a sympathetic attempt to exterminate the insurgents? When, during the French Revolution, the French people overthrew kings and aristocrats, did not all the feudal lords and rulers of Europe take sympathetic action to restore the French monarchy, even although doing it involved throwing all industrial life in Europe into chaos and drenching a Continent with blood?

Historically, the sympathetic strike can find ample justification. But, and this point must be emphasised, it was not mere cool reasoning that gave it birth in Dublin. In this city, it was born out of our desperate necessity. Seeing all classes of semi-skilled labour in Dublin so wretchedly underpaid and so atrociously sweated, the Irish Transport and General Workers' Union taught them to stand together and help one another, and out of this advice the more perfect weapon has grown. That the Labour movement here has utilised it before elsewhere is due to the fact that in this city what is known as general or unskilled labour bears a greater proportion to the whole body of workers than elsewhere. And hence the workers are a more moveable, fluctuating body, are more often as individuals engaged in totally dissimilar industries than in the English cities, where skilled trades absorb so great a proportion, and keep them so long in the one class of industry.

Out of all this turmoil and fighting the Union has evolved, is evolving, among its members a higher conception of mutual life, a realisation of their duties to each other and to society at large, and are thus building for the future in a way that ought to gladden the hearts of all lovers of the race. In contrast to the narrow, restricted outlook of the capitalist class, and even of certain old-fashioned trade-unionism, with their perpetual insistence upon "rights," this union insists, almost fiercely, that there are no rights without duties, and the first duty is to help one another. This is indeed revolutionary and disturbing, but not half as much as would be a practical following out of the moral precepts of Christianity.

For the immediate present, the way out of this deadlock is for all sides to consent to the formation of a Conciliation Board, before which all disputes must be brought. Let the employers insist upon levelling up the conditions of employment to one high standard; treat as an Ishmael any employer who refuses to conform, and leave him unassisted to fight the battle with the Union; let the Union proceed to organise all the workers possible, place all disputes as to wages before the Board for discussion, and only resort to a strike when agreement cannot be reached by the Board; and as all employers would be interested in bringing the more obdurate and greedy to reason, strikes would be rare. And when strikes were rare, the necessity for sympathetic strikes would also seldom develop.

Thus we will develop a social conscience, and lay the foundation for an orderly transformation of society in the future into a more perfect and a juster social order.

The Dublin Lock Out:
On the Eve

First Published in *The Irish Review*
October 1913, Vol. 3, No. 32

James Connolly

Perhaps before this issue of *The Irish Worker* is in the hands of its readers the issues now at stake in Dublin will be brought to a final determination. All the capitalist newspapers of Friday last join in urging, or giving favourable publicity to the views of others urging the employers of Dublin to join in a general lock-out of the members of the Irish Transport and General Workers' Union. It is as well. Possibly some such act is necessary in order to make that portion of the working class which still halts undecided to understand dearly what it is that lies behind the tyrannical and brow-beating attitude of the proprietors of the Dublin tramway system.

The fault of the Irish Transport and General Workers' Union! What is it? Let us tell it in plain language. Its fault is this, that it found the labourers of Ireland on their knees, and has striven to raise them to the erect position of manhood; it found them with all the vices of slavery in their souls, and it strove to eradicate these vices and replace them with some of the virtues of free men; it found them with no other weapons of defence than the arts of the liar, the lickspittle, and the toady, and it combined them and taught them to abhor those arts and rely proudly on the defensive power of combination; it, in short, found a class in whom seven centuries of social outlawry had added fresh degradations upon the burden it bore as the members of a nation suffering from the cumulative effects of seven centuries of national bondage, and out of this class, the degraded slaves of slaves more degraded still—for what degradation is more abysmal than that of those who prostitute their manhood on the altar of profit-mongering?—out of this class of slaves the labourers of Dublin, the Irish Transport and General Workers' Union has created an army of intelligent self-reliant men, abhorring the old arts of the toady, the lickspittle, and the crawler and trusting alone to the disciplined use of their power to labour or to withdraw their labour to assert and maintain their right as men.

To put it in other words, but words as pregnant with truth and meaning: the Irish Transport and General Workers' Union found that before its advent the working class of Dublin had been taught by all the educational agencies of the country, by all the social influences of their masters, that this world was created for the special benefit of the various sections of the master class, that kings and lords and capitalists were of value; that even flunkeys, toadies, lickspittle and poodle dogs had an honoured place in the scheme of the universe, but that there was neither honour, credit, nor consideration to the man or woman who toils to maintain them all.

Against all this the Irish Transport and General Workers' Union has taught that they who toil are the only ones that do matter, that all others are but beggars upon the bounty of those who work with hand or brain, and that this superiority of social value can at any time be realised, be translated into actual fact, by the combination of the labouring class. Preaching, organising, and fighting upon this basis, the Irish Transport and General Workers' Union has done what? If the value of a city is to be found in the development of self-respect and high conception of social responsibilities among a people, then the Irish Transport and General Workers' Union found Dublin the poorest city in these countries by reason of its lack of these qualities. And by imbuing the workers with them, it has made Dublin the richest city in Europe today, rich by all that counts for greatness in the history of nations.

It is then upon this working class so enslaved, this working class so led and so enriched with moral purposes and high aims that the employers propose to make general war. Shall we shrink from it; cower before their onset? A thousand times no! Shall we crawl back into our slums, abase our hearts, bow our knees, and crawl once more to lick the hand that would smite us? Shall we, who have been carving out for our children a brighter future, a cleaner city, a freer life, consent to betray them instead into the grasp of the blood-suckers from whom we have dreamt of escaping? No, no, and yet again no!

Let them declare their lock-out; it will only hasten the day when the working class will lockout the capitalist class for good and all. If for taking the side of the Tram men we are threatened with suffering, why we have suffered before. But let them understand well that once they start that ball rolling no capitalist power on earth can prevent it continuing to roll, that every day will add to the impetus it will give to the working class purpose, to the thousands it will bring to the working class ranks and every added suffering inflicted upon the workers will be a fresh obstacle in the way of moderation when the day of final settlement arrives.

Yes, indeed, if it is going to be a wedding, let it be a wedding; and if it is going to be a wake, let it be a wake: we are ready for either.

NOTES: